Table of Contents

CARING FOR SPIDER MONKEY

A HANDBOOK GUIDE IN OWNING A PET SPIDER MONKEY

DR HUNTER DAVIS

An Overview of Pet Spider Monkeys

Mostly found in the wild, but some devoted enthusiasts have kept some as pets, spider monkeys are fascinating and charismatic primates native to the lush forests of Central and South America. Known for their long limbs, prehensile tails, and expressive faces, these intelligent creatures have captured the imagination of humans for centuries.

This introduction is meant to act as a roadmap for anyone thinking about embarking on the extraordinary journey of owning a spider monkey. It explores the intricacies and obligations that come with taking care of these extraordinary creatures, stressing the significance of comprehending their innate tendencies, unique requirements, and the moral dilemmas that come with owning them.

We'll explore the benefits and drawbacks of living with a spider monkey while offering insightful information on their upkeep, enrichment, health, and legal issues. At the conclusion of this journey, you'll have a thorough grasp of all that it takes to bring a spider monkey into your home and begin a rewarding and enriching relationship with one of nature's most fascinating animals.

Chapter 1

Recognizing the Needs and Behavior of Spider Monkeys

With their long limbs, slender bodies, and prehensile tails, spider monkeys are some of the most fascinating and mysterious animals in the animal kingdom. These primates are native to the dense rainforests of Central and South America, and they have a wide range of behaviors and special needs that anyone thinking about getting a pet needs to understand. In this extensive guide, we will go into great detail about the peculiarities of spider monkey behavior and the needs that are unique to them.

Patterns of Behavior:

Given that they are highly social animals and usually live in large groups called troops, it is important to understand the social dynamics of spider monkeys in order to provide them with appropriate companionship and prevent potential conflicts in captivity. Spider monkeys exhibit complex social structures within their troops, with hierarchical arrangements that influence their interactions and dynamics.

Interaction:

Building trust and promoting positive interactions with pet spider monkeys requires an understanding of the three main forms of communication used by these primates: vocalizations, body language, and facial expressions. Spider monkeys use vocalizations to convey different messages, such as alarm calls, mating calls, and territorial calls; they also rely on body postures and facial expressions to express emotions and intentions, such as dominance, submission, or aggression.

Feeding Patterns:

As frugivores, spider monkeys mostly eat fruits, with occasional insects, leaves, seeds, and flowers as supplements. Their diet is high in fiber, vitamins, and minerals, all of which are necessary for their general health and well-being. In captivity, it is important to mimic their natural diet in order to meet their nutritional needs and avoid health problems related to diet. It is also important to provide a variety of fresh fruits and vegetables to ensure that their dietary needs are met.

Gathering food:

Because of their prehensile tails, which are essential for both locomotion and foraging, spider monkeys are expert foragers who spend a large amount of their time in the forest canopy searching for food. Encouraging natural foraging behaviors in captivity through enrichment activities like puzzle feeders and food scatterings helps stimulate their minds and provide mental stimulation.

Physical activity and exercise:

As they swing and leap through the trees in search of food and mates, spider monkeys in captivity need plenty of room and physical exercise to stay physically healthy and avoid boredom. Giving captive spider monkeys spacious, well-equipped enclosures with climbing frames, ropes, and platforms allows them to exercise their bodies and participate in natural behaviors.

Enhancement of the Environment:

Enrichment activities can include new objects, puzzles, foraging opportunities, and social interactions. Rotating enrichment regularly prevents habituation and ensures continued engagement and stimulation for pet spider monkeys. Enrichment plays a crucial role in enhancing the well-being of captive spider monkeys by providing mental stimulation, promoting physical activity, and satisfying their natural instincts.

Getting Along:

Because they are inherently gregarious and prefer the company of their own species, spider monkeys need opportunities for socialization with other members of their own species. Whenever possible, it is best to provide spider monkeys with companionship from individuals who are compatible with them in order to prevent loneliness and promote psychological well-being.

Enhancement of Cognitive Function:

Training sessions, puzzle feeders, and interactive games are excellent ways to challenge spider monkeys' cognitive abilities and promote learning. Spider monkeys are intelligent creatures with complex cognitive abilities, including problem-solving, tool use, and social learning. Including cognitive enrichment activities into their daily routine stimulates their minds and provides opportunities for mental stimulation and engagement.

Health Care:

A balanced diet, good hygiene, and a clean living environment reduce the risk of infectious diseases and ensure optimal health for captive spider monkeys. Regular veterinary care is crucial for maintaining the health and well-being of pet spider monkeys. Vaccinations, check-ups, and preventive measures help identify and address potential health issues early on.

A Legal and Ethical Perspective:
Aside from the fact that owning a pet spider monkey entails certain legal and ethical obligations, owning a

spider monkey as a pet can also involve ethical considerations regarding the welfare and conservation of these animals, as many spider monkeys are protected species and ownership may be subject to stringent regulations and permits.

Comprehending the behavior and needs of spider monkeys is crucial to giving them the care and stimulation they need to flourish in captivity. Through learning about these amazing creatures' social dynamics, cues for communication, food preferences, and enrichment needs, pet owners can create a nurturing environment that supports the physical, mental, and emotional health of their pets. With the right care, attention, and commitment, living with a spider monkey can be fulfilling and enriching for both the human and the animal.

Chapter 2

Creating the Perfect Setting with Enclosures and Enrichment

A spider monkey's physical and mental health depend on the environment they live in, so it's important to create the best possible conditions for them. In this extensive guide, we will go over the essential elements of building an appropriate enclosure and putting into practice enrichment techniques that enhance the health and happiness of spider monkey pets. From comprehending their natural habitat to creating stimulating environments, we'll cover everything you need to know to give these amazing creatures the best care possible.

Knowing the Habitat of Spider Monkeys:

In order to meet the physical and behavioral needs of spider monkeys, it is imperative to replicate elements of their natural habitat in captivity. Spider monkeys are endemic to the dense rainforests of Central and South America, where they live in the upper canopy layers of the forest and are characterized by tall trees, dense foliage, and a rich diversity of plant and animal life.

Design of Enclosures:

Prioritizing space, safety, and complexity are crucial when designing an enclosure for a spider monkey. Ideally, the enclosure should be large enough to accommodate natural behaviors like swinging, climbing, and exploring. It should also be secure to keep the monkey from escaping and shield it from potential threats.

Vertical Room:

Since spider monkeys are arboreal animals and spend most of their time in treetops, enclosures should have vertical space so that the monkeys can engage in natural behaviors like climbing and swinging. Tall structures like trees, poles, and platforms can be used to provide spider monkeys with plenty of space to move around and practice their climbing skills.

Horizontal Area:

Spider monkeys need plenty of room to move around and explore both vertically and horizontally. If they are kept in a group, enclosures should be big enough to hold several individuals so they can maintain social interactions and establish territories. Adding a variety of branches, pathways, and perches makes the environment more complex and promotes natural behaviors.

Naturalistic Components:

Live plants, branches, and vines are examples of naturalistic elements that can be added to an enclosure to give spider monkeys a more stimulating and enriching environment. These elements mimic aspects of the monkeys' natural habitat and provide opportunities for exploration, foraging, and sensory stimulation.

Safety Observations:

When designing an enclosure, the safety of the spider monkey and its human caregivers should always come first. Materials used in the enclosure design should be non-toxic and strong enough to withstand the strength and agility of the monkey. In order to prevent escapes by accident or unauthorized access, enclosures should also be equipped with secure locks and escape-proof barriers.

Strategies for Enrichment:

Utilizing a range of enrichment strategies helps prevent boredom and encourages natural behaviors, which in turn improves the quality of life for captive spider monkeys by satisfying their natural instincts, stimulating their minds, and encouraging physical activity.

Conundrum Feeders:

Foraging balls, Kong toys, and food puzzles are a few examples of interactive puzzle feeders that require the monkey to manipulate objects in order to access food rewards. These feeders slow down feeding and prevent boredom while also stimulating problem-solving abilities and mental stimulation.

Environmental Deception:

Rotating enrichment regularly prevents habituation and ensures continued engagement and stimulation. Changing elements of the enclosure, such as moving furniture, adding new objects, or changing the layout of the enclosure, provides novelty and unpredictability, stimulating the monkey's curiosity and promoting exploration.

Enhancing Social Relations:

The psychological well-being of spider monkeys depends on providing opportunities for social interaction and companionship; if a single monkey is kept, regular supervised play sessions with compatible individuals or the introduction of a mirror for social stimulation can help prevent loneliness. Spider monkeys are highly social animals that thrive in the company of conspecifics.

Instruction and Enhancement of Cognition:

Teaching basic commands and participating in cognitive enrichment activities like memory games, problem-solving tasks, and object discrimination exercises challenges the monkey's cognitive abilities and strengthens the bond between the monkey and its caregivers. Training sessions offer mental stimulation and promote positive interactions between the monkey and its caregivers.

Enhancement of Senses:

Encouraging the monkeys' senses with auditory, olfactory, and tactile enrichment activities improves their overall happiness and well-being. Giving them the chance to explore various textures and scents, play in water or take sand baths, and listen to natural sounds also helps to stimulate their minds.

A spider monkey's natural habitat should be carefully considered, as should enclosure design, safety issues, and enrichment techniques. Pet owners can guarantee the health, happiness, and well-being of their spider monkey companions by providing a large, stimulating, and safe environment that is tailored to their specific needs. Living with a spider monkey can be a rewarding and enriching experience for both the animal and its human caregivers and can be achieved with commitment, creativity, and a thorough understanding of their natural behaviors.

Chapter 3

How to Feed a Spider Monkey: Nutrition and Diet

In order to maintain optimal health and longevity, spider monkeys kept in captivity require proper nutrition. Because they are frugivores, there are specific dietary requirements that must be met. In this extensive guide, we will explore the natural diet, nutritional requirements, and best practices for providing a balanced and enriching diet for spider monkeys in captivity.

Comprehending Spider Monkeys' Natural Diet:

In their natural environment, spider monkeys mostly eat fruits, with occasional insects, leaves, seeds, and flowers rounding out their diet. Fruits provide important nutrients like vitamins, minerals, and carbohydrates, and their diets are generally low in fat and high in fiber because of the abundance of fruits and foliage in their tropical forest.

The necessary nutrients:

A balanced diet for pet spider monkeys should include a variety of fruits, vegetables, nuts, seeds, and protein sources. Providing a diverse assortment of foods ensures that they receive all the essential nutrients they need to thrive. Spider monkeys have specific nutritional requirements that must be met to maintain their health and well-being in captivity.

Fruits:

Since fruits are the main food source in a spider monkey's natural habitat, they provide a wide variety of fruits, including bananas, apples, oranges, grapes, berries, mangoes, and papayas. Fruits with high acidity or high sugar content, like grapes and citrus fruits, should not be fed in excess as they can lead to digestive problems.

Produce:

Offer a variety of leafy greens, root vegetables, and cruciferous vegetables, such as kale, spinach, carrots, broccoli, and bell peppers. Rotate the selection frequently to provide variety and prevent boredom. Vegetables are an important source of vitamins, minerals, and fiber for spider monkeys.

Seeds and Nuts:

Nuts and seeds are foods high in nutrients that supply important fats, proteins, and micronutrients. Since nuts and seeds are high in calories and fat, give them in moderation as treats. Nuts and seeds that work well for this include almonds, walnuts, pecans, sunflower seeds, and pumpkin seeds.

Sources of Protein:

Spider monkeys can obtain their protein from insects, eggs, and legumes; include small amounts of cooked eggs, mealworms, crickets, and beans in their diet. Protein should be provided in moderation and should be complemented with plant-based sources to avoid excessive fat intake.

Addenda:

Consult a veterinarian or nutritionist to determine the appropriate supplementation regimen for your spider monkey. Supplements may be necessary to ensure that spider monkeys receive all the essential nutrients they need. Calcium and vitamin D3 supplements are particularly important for maintaining bone health and preventing nutritional deficiencies.

Drinking plenty of water

Spider monkeys need to be well hydrated, so make sure they always have access to clean, fresh water. You can also encourage regular drinking by providing fruits and vegetables that are high in water. Keep a close eye on their water intake because dehydration can quickly cause major health problems.

Feeding Timetable:

Offering small, frequent meals throughout the day to mimic their natural feeding patterns is an important way to maintain proper nutrition and prevent obesity or malnutrition. You should also monitor their appetite and adjust portion sizes accordingly to ensure they are consuming an appropriate amount of food.

Extra Attention to Detail

Age, health, and personal preferences can all influence a spider monkey's dietary needs, so pay close attention to what they eat and adjust as necessary to suit their needs. You should also be aware of any allergies or sensitivities they may have to avoid giving them potentially harmful foods.

Making the Switch to a New Diet:

Introduce new foods gradually over several days or weeks, gradually increasing the portion size as they become accustomed to the changes, and monitor their response to new foods for any signs of intolerance or allergic reactions. This will help to prevent upset stomachs and avoid any signs of intolerance or allergic reactions.

A balanced and nutritious diet is vital for a spider monkey's health, happiness, and general well-being when kept in captivity. Pet owners can provide their spider monkey companions a diet that supports their physiological needs and promotes their general health by learning about their natural dietary preferences, nutritional requirements, and best feeding practices. Living with a spider monkey can be a fulfilling and enriching experience for both the animal and its human caregivers when they provide the necessary care and attention.

Chapter 4

Spider Monkey Health and Veterinary Care

As with any exotic pet, spider monkeys are prone to a range of health problems that may arise in a captive setting. In this comprehensive guide, we will explore the significance of veterinary care, common health concerns, preventive measures, and best practices for promoting the overall health and longevity of pet spider monkeys.

The Value of Veterinary Treatment

A licensed exotic animal veterinarian with experience in primate medicine should perform routine check-ups and provide preventive care to ensure the well-being of captive spider monkeys. Veterinary visits also provide opportunities for health screenings, vaccinations, and parasite control. Regular veterinary care is essential for monitoring the health status of spider monkeys and addressing any medical concerns in a timely manner.

Normal Health Examinations:

Regular health examinations allow veterinarians to detect and address health issues early, before they escalate into more serious problems. A comprehensive physical assessment, evaluation of the monkey's body condition, check for signs of illness or injury, and assessment of overall well-being are all part of routine preventive veterinary care for spider monkeys.

Immunizations:

In order to safeguard spider monkeys from infectious diseases that could endanger their health, vaccinations are essential. Depending on their geographic location and possible exposure risks, spider monkeys may need to be vaccinated against diseases like rabies, hepatitis, and tetanus. Speak with a veterinarian to create a vaccination schedule that is customized for your spider monkey.

Manage Parasites:

Veterinarians may suggest periodic deworming treatments and topical or oral medications to control external parasites. Intestinal worms, mites, and ticks are examples of parasites that can pose health risks and compromise the well-being of spider monkeys. Establishing a regular parasite control program is crucial for preventing infestations and maintaining the health of captive spider monkeys.

Dietary counseling and nutrition assessment:

A balanced and nutritious diet is essential for supporting the health, growth, and vitality of captive spider monkeys. Veterinarians can evaluate the monkeys' dietary intake, assess their nutritional status, and provide guidance on feeding practices and dietary supplementation. Nutritional assessment and dietary counseling are crucial components of veterinary care for spider monkeys.

Testing for Diagnosis:

Diagnostic tests, which aid veterinarians in identifying health issues, tracking the progression of diseases, and guiding treatment decisions, may be required to assess the health status of spider monkeys and diagnose underlying medical conditions. Common diagnostic tests include blood tests, fecal examinations, imaging studies (such as X-rays or ultrasounds), and microbiological cultures.

Assessment of Behavior:

Veterinarians can evaluate the behavior of spider monkeys, watch for signs of stress or anxiety, and recommend environmental enrichment and behavioral management strategies to support their well-being. Behavioral evaluation is an essential part of veterinary care for spider monkeys because behavioral changes can reveal underlying health issues or psychological distress.

Emergency Medical Attention:

Establishing a relationship with an emergency veterinary clinic or primate rescue center equipped to handle exotic animal emergencies is advised. Pet owners should also familiarize themselves with common signs of illness or injury and know how to respond appropriately in emergency situations. In the event of a medical emergency, timely veterinary intervention is essential to ensuring the health and safety of spider monkeys.

Typical Health Concerns:

Spider monkeys are susceptible to a range of health problems that are frequently seen in captivity. These problems can include respiratory infections, gastrointestinal disorders, dental issues, parasitic infestations, and metabolic disorders. The best way to treat and manage these health issues is to recognize the warning signs and symptoms and seek veterinary care as soon as possible.

Infected respiratory systems:

Coughing, sneezing, nasal discharge, difficulty breathing, and lethargy are some of the symptoms of respiratory infections, which are common in captive primates, including spider monkeys. Prompt veterinary evaluation and treatment with antibiotics or antifungal medications are necessary to prevent complications and promote recovery.

Digestive System Disorders:

Spider monkeys can develop gastrointestinal disorders, such as diarrhea, constipation, and bloating, as a result of dietary errors, bacterial infections, or parasitic infestations. It is important to monitor the monkeys' fecal output, consistency, and frequency in order to identify gastrointestinal problems early on. Interventions such as supportive care, medication, and dietary changes may be required in order to address gastrointestinal problems and restore normal bowel function.

Dental issues

In order to effectively address dental problems, veterinarians may recommend dental cleanings, extractions, or corrective procedures. Dental problems, such as dental decay, periodontal disease, and malocclusions, are common in captive primates and can cause pain, discomfort, and difficulty eating. Regular dental examinations and preventive dental care are essential for maintaining oral health and preventing dental issues in spider monkeys.

Infestations of Parasites:

Veterinarians may suggest deworming medications, topical insecticides, or environmental treatments to effectively eradicate parasites. Parasitic infestations, such as intestinal worms, mites, and ticks, are common in captive spider monkeys and can cause a variety of health problems if left untreated. Regular parasite screenings and preventive treatments are essential for controlling parasites and minimizing their impact on the monkey's health.

Disorders of the Metabolism:

For this reason, it is important to monitor the monkeys' body condition, weight, and dietary intake in order to prevent metabolic disorders and maintain optimal health. Dietary modifications, exercise, and medical management may be necessary to address metabolic issues and promote weight loss or nutritional balance. Metabolic disorders, including obesity, diabetes, and vitamin deficiencies, can occur in captive spider monkeys due to inappropriate diet, lack of exercise, or underlying health conditions.

Preventive actions:

In addition to routine veterinary care, pet owners can implement various preventive measures to maintain the health and vitality of their monkey companions. Preventive measures are essential for minimizing the risk of health problems and promoting the overall well-being of captive spider monkeys.

Dietary Management: To support the health of spider monkeys and prevent nutritional deficiencies, provide a balanced and nutritious diet specific to their needs. Work with a veterinarian or nutritionist to create a diet plan that satisfies the monkeys' nutritional needs and enhances their general well-being.

Provide a variety of enrichment devices, toys, and activities to keep the monkey engaged and stimulated. Environmental Enrichment: Enhancing the monkey's surroundings with stimulating activities, social interactions, and opportunities for natural behaviors promotes mental and emotional well-being and reduces stress and boredom.

Hygiene and tidiness: Keeping the monkey's living space clean and hygienic minimizes exposure to pathogens and aids in the prevention of infectious disease transmission. To lower the risk of contamination, routinely clean and disinfect the enclosure, feeding dishes, and water bowls.

Frequent Exercise: Spider monkeys benefit from regular exercise because it keeps them lean and prevents muscle atrophy and obesity. It also stimulates their minds by allowing them to engage in natural activities like swinging, climbing, and exploring.

Providing opportunities for social interaction and companionship with compatible individuals helps prevent loneliness and promotes overall well-being. If you are keeping a single monkey, set up regular play sessions or introduce a mirror for social stimulation. Spider monkeys are highly social animals that thrive in the company of conspecifics.

Proper care and attention, along with a dedication to providing a nurturing environment, can make living with a spider monkey rewarding and enriching for both the animal and its human caregivers. Proactive veterinary care, preventive measures, and a commitment to meeting the physical and emotional needs of spider monkeys are all necessary to ensure their health and well-being in captivity. Pet owners can promote the health, happiness, and longevity of their spider monkey companions by developing a relationship with a qualified exotic animal veterinarian, keeping a close eye on their health, and putting preventive measures in place.

Chapter 5

Activities to Train and Enrich Spider Monkeys

For spider monkeys housed in captivity, training and enrichment activities are essential to their physical, mental, and emotional health. Owners of monkeys can stimulate their pets, encourage natural behaviors, and fortify the bond between humans and primates by offering structured training sessions and a range of enriching experiences. We will examine training principles, successful enrichment techniques, and best practices for creating an environment that is both stimulating and fulfilling for captive spider monkeys in this extensive guide.

Comprehending the Fundamentals of Training:
In order to teach desired behaviors and promote cooperation in spider monkey training, positive

reinforcement techniques are used instead of coercion or punishment. Giving the monkey a favorite object or activity right away after they exhibit the desired behavior is known as positive reinforcement, and it makes the behavior more likely to happen again in the future. Effective training outcomes depend on patience, consistency, and clear communication.

Fundamental Commands for Training:

Behavioral management, medical procedures, and husbandry tasks can all be facilitated by teaching spider monkeys to obey simple commands. Common commands include "come," "sit," "stay," "down," and "target." Pet owners can create clear communication channels and encourage cooperative behaviors by teaching these commands using positive reinforcement training techniques.

Objective Instruction:

Teaching a monkey to touch or follow a specific target—such as a stick or a hand-held object—is known as target training. Target training is an adaptable method that can be used to teach recall, shifting, and stationing, among other behaviors. Pet owners can effectively guide and shape their monkey's behavior by using a target as a visual cue.

Training in Crates:

Acclimating a monkey to a transport crate or enclosure for stress-free, secure travel is known as crate training. It is best to introduce crate training gradually and use positive reinforcement methods to help the monkey get into and stay calm inside the crate. Pet owners can reduce anxiety and increase the comfort level of their monkeys during crate time by associating the crate with positive experiences and rewards.

Strategies for Positive Reinforcement:

When a monkey engages in desired behavior, positive reinforcement techniques are used to immediately reward them with preferred objects or activities. Incentives can take the form of toys, food treats, compliments, or opportunities to socialize. When employing positive reinforcement, timing is essential because, in order to effectively reinforce the association, the reward should be given right after the desired behavior.

Clicker Instruction:

A portable clicker device is used in clicker training, a well-liked technique for positive reinforcement training, to mark desired behaviors. When the monkey performs the appropriate behavior, the clicker makes a distinctive sound to let them know they will be rewarded. Clicker training is a useful tool for learning facilitation and behavior modification because it enables accurate timing and clear communication.

Counterconditioning and Desensitization:

Spider monkeys can be trained to overcome fear, anxiety, or aversion to particular stimuli or situations by using desensitization and counterconditioning techniques. Pet owners can help monkeys learn to associate a feared stimulus with positive experiences and lessen their fear or anxiety response by introducing them to it gradually in a controlled and positive way and pairing it with rewards.

Strategies for Enrichment:

For captive spider monkeys to maintain their natural behaviors, receive mental stimulation, and avoid boredom, enrichment activities are crucial. Diverse, species-specific, and catered to each monkey's unique preferences and abilities, enrichment should be provided. Pet owners can provide a stimulating environment and improve the quality of life for their monkeys by implementing various enrichment strategies into their daily routine.

Enhancement of the Physical Domain:

The monkey is encouraged to participate in natural behaviors like climbing, swinging, and exploring through physical enrichment activities. By providing climbing frames, ropes, ladders, and platforms, physical fitness is encouraged while the monkey exercises strength and agility. Regularly changing the enclosure's layout and adding new elements, like obstacles or objects, promotes exploration and keeps people from growing accustomed to it.

Enhancement through Foraging:

In addition to providing mental stimulation, foraging enrichment activities encourage the monkeys' innate foraging instincts. When food is scattered, hidden in puzzle feeders or other foraging tools, or hidden in unexpected places, the monkey is encouraged to explore, manipulate, and solve problems in order to find and retrieve their food rewards. In addition to meeting the monkeys' nutritional needs, foraging enrichment encourages mental engagement and keeps them from getting bored.

Enhancing Social Relations:

Activities that promote social enrichment offer chances for companionship and social interaction with human caregivers or conspecifics. If maintaining a single monkey isn't possible, setting up supervised playdates with matched people or adding a mirror to encourage social interaction can help avoid loneliness and advance wellbeing. The monkey's relationship with its human companions is further reinforced by positive social interactions with familiar caregivers.

Enhancement of Cognitive Function:

The cognitive capacities of the monkey are tested and mental stimulation is encouraged through cognitive enrichment activities. The monkey is encouraged to use their intelligence, memory, and problem-solving abilities to obtain rewards through training sessions, puzzle feeders, interactive toys, and problem-solving tasks. Cognitive enrichment activities promote learning and skill development, keep people from getting bored, and provide mental stimulation.

Enhancement of Senses:

Activities that provide opportunities for exploration and sensory stimulation stimulate the monkeys' senses. Encouraging children to partake in sensory baths or water play, investigate various textures and scents, and listen to nature's sounds enhances their sensory experiences and stimulates their minds. Activities that provide sensory enrichment are novel and varied, which helps to avoid habituation and enhance wellbeing.

Enhancement of the Environment:

By altering the monkeys' living quarters, environmental enrichment aims to stimulate their minds and bodies while also fostering natural behaviors and exploration. A dynamic and stimulating environment is created by offering a range of substrates, climbing structures, hiding places, and perches, which encourages the monkey to engage in natural behaviors and investigate their surroundings.

Interactive Improvement:

The monkey participates in interactive play or training sessions with human caregivers as part of interactive enrichment activities. In addition to offering mental and physical stimulation, teaching new behaviors, engaging in games, or attending organized training sessions help to fortify the relationship between the monkey and its human companion. Engaging in interactive enrichment activities facilitates learning, positive reinforcement, and socialization.

Giving captivity-housed spider monkeys an environment that is both stimulating and fulfilling requires both training and enrichment activities. Pet owners can support natural behaviors, fortify the bond between humans and primates, and improve the general wellbeing of their monkey companions by introducing positive reinforcement training methods and a range of enriching experiences into their daily routine. Living with a spider monkey can be a fulfilling and enriching experience for both the animal and its human caregivers if you have the patience, creativity, and dedication to meet their physical and emotional needs.

Chapter 6

Developing a Strong Bond and Socialization with Spider Monkeys

The two most important aspects of providing care for captivity-bred spider monkeys are bonding and socialization. Building a solid bond with these social and intellectual primates that is founded on mutual respect, trust, and positive interactions is crucial to supporting their mental, emotional, and physical health. We will go over the fundamentals of bonding and socialization, practical methods for creating a solid rapport, and best practices for encouraging camaraderie and trust between spider monkeys and their human caregivers in this extensive guide.

Comprehending Social Behavior of Spider Monkeys:

Spider monkeys are extremely gregarious creatures that reside in intricate social units called troops. They participate in a range of social activities within these troops, such as playing, grooming, interacting, and developing close social ties with conspecifics. In order to provide suitable companionship and socialization opportunities for spider monkeys kept in captivity, it is imperative to comprehend their social behavior.

Social Organization:

Spider monkey troops, which are made up of several females, juveniles, and babies, are usually led by a dominant male. People in the troop establish strong social ties and uphold complex social hierarchies, which affect how they interact and behave. To satisfy the social needs of pet spider monkeys, a comparable social structure with chances for companionship and socialization must be established in captivity.

Social Communication:

Spider monkey behavior and well-being are greatly influenced by social interaction, which offers chances for cooperation, bonding, and communication. To build a stronger bond and promote a sense of trust and security, pet owners should actively engage with their spider monkey companions through positive interactions, play sessions, and shared activities.

Interaction:

Building a solid relationship with a companion spider monkey requires open communication. Spider monkeys express a variety of emotions, intentions, and social cues through their vocalizations, body language, and facial expressions. Pet owners can develop a relationship and mutual understanding with their monkey companions by learning to read their cues and react accordingly.

Establishing a Solid Bond:

Strong relationships with spider monkeys need to be developed over time with persistence, patience, and consistent effort. Pet owners can help their monkey companions develop trust, cooperation, and companionship by implementing positive reinforcement techniques, socialization opportunities, and mutual respect into their interactions. The relationships between spider monkeys and their human caretakers can be strengthened by implementing the following tactics:

Encouragement that is constructive:

In order to reinforce desired behaviors, positive reinforcement involves providing treats, praise, or preferred activities. Pet owners can promote cooperation and strengthen their relationship with their monkeys by rewarding them for exhibiting desired behaviors like responding to calls, sitting quietly, or taking part in training sessions.

Building Trust Activities:

Activities aimed at developing rapport and trust between the monkey and its human caregivers are called trust-building exercises. Gentle grooming sessions, giving favorite foods or treats by hand, or participating in interactive play or training sessions are a few examples of these exercises. Pet owners can develop a stronger relationship and foster trust with their monkey companions by fostering positive associations and experiences.

Opportunities for Socialization:

It is crucial to provide spider monkeys with socialization opportunities with their conspecifics or human caregivers in order to satisfy their social needs. If maintaining a single monkey isn't possible, setting up supervised playdates with matched people or adding a mirror to encourage social interaction can help avoid loneliness and advance wellbeing. The monkey's relationship with its human companions is further reinforced by positive social interactions with familiar caregivers.

Collaborative Tasks:

The relationship between spider monkeys and their human caretakers is strengthened when they participate in shared experiences and activities. Grooming, feeding, training, and interactive play are examples of activities that foster cooperation, enjoyment, and communication between participants. Regularly engaging in activities together can help pet owners and their monkey companions develop a sense of camaraderie and connection.

courtesy and comprehension

Establishing a robust bond with a companion spider monkey requires mutual respect and comprehension. When interacting with a monkey, pet owners should respect its autonomy, preferences, and boundaries and refrain from using force or coercion. Pet owners may develop mutual respect and trust in their relationship with monkeys by paying attention to their behavior, picking up on their communication cues, and reacting sympathetically.

Consistency and Patience:

The foundation of a solid relationship with a spider monkey companion is patience and consistency.

Establishing rapport and trust takes time, and development may be sluggish. Pet owners ought to be understanding and patient, letting the monkey get used to them and gain confidence at its own speed. Clear communication is established and cooperation and trust are encouraged through the use of consistent training methods, routines, and expectations.

Developing Self-Belief:

Developing self-confidence is crucial to supporting spider monkeys' independence and general well-being in captivity. Through facilitating exploration, problem-solving, and skill acquisition, pet owners can contribute to the development of their monkey's resilience and self-assurance. The monkey gains confidence and empowerment when he is encouraged to try new things, face his fears, and overcome challenges.

Controlling Anxiety and Fear:

For the sake of fostering the wellbeing of spider monkeys kept in captivity, fear and anxiety management is essential. Pet owners can help reduce anxiety and foster trust and confidence in their relationship with their monkeys by providing a safe and predictable environment, exposing the monkey to feared stimuli gradually, and offering reassurance and support. Managing fear-based behaviors in spider monkeys requires a great deal of tolerance, compassion, and understanding.

Handling Dominance and Aggression:

Maintaining a harmonious relationship between spider monkeys and their human caregivers requires addressing aggression and dominance behaviors. Pet owners can prevent aggression and encourage polite interactions by setting clear boundaries, enforcing rules consistently, and redirecting undesirable behaviors with positive reinforcement techniques. To effectively address more complex behavior issues, consulting with a qualified veterinarian or animal behaviorist may be necessary.

Providing care for spider monkeys housed in captivity requires both bonding and socialization. Pet owners can support their monkey companions' physical, mental, and emotional well-being by building a solid relationship based on mutual respect, trust, and positive interactions. Pet owners may develop a strong and meaningful bond with their spider monkey companions by implementing positive reinforcement methods, socialization opportunities, and mutual understanding into their interactions. Living with a spider monkey can be a fulfilling and enriching experience for both the animal and its human caregivers if you have the necessary patience, empathy, and dedication to fostering a positive relationship.

Chapter 7

Legal Aspects and Ethical Obligations in Keeping Pet Spider Monkeys

Pet owners who keep spider monkeys as pets have moral and legal obligations that they must follow to guarantee the wellbeing and safety of these unusual creatures. Because they are social and highly intelligent animals, spider monkeys need particular housing and care in order to flourish in captivity. We will examine the ethical issues surrounding the welfare of spider monkeys, the legal framework governing their ownership, and best practices for ethical ownership and advocacy on behalf of these amazing primates in this extensive guide.

Lawful Structure:

Depending on the jurisdiction, different laws may apply to the possession and upkeep of spider monkeys. These laws may include municipal, state/provincial, and federal regulations. It is imperative that individuals considering becoming pet owners become knowledgeable about the applicable laws and rules that control the ownership, trade, and transit of exotic animals, such as spider monkeys. Common legal factors to think about could be:

Licenses and Permits: Owning exotic animals, such as spider monkeys, requires a license or permit in many places. Departments of Agriculture, Wildlife Agencies, or Animal Control Authorities may issue these permits. In order to lawfully own and take care of spider monkeys, pet owners must obtain the required permits and adhere to regulatory requirements.

Zoning laws: In certain towns or residential zones, owning exotic animals may be prohibited by zoning laws.

To make sure they are in compliance with any laws prohibiting the keeping of spider monkeys as pets, pet owners should review their local zoning ordinances and homeowners association rules.

Regulations Governing Import and Export: International treaties, such as the Convention on International Trade in Endangered Species of Wild Fauna and Flora (CITES), may apply to the import and export of spider monkeys. To ensure the conservation and protection of threatened and endangered species, such as spider monkeys, CITES regulates their trade. A valid permit and the necessary paperwork are required when bringing spider monkeys across international borders.

Animal Welfare Laws: The treatment and care of animals, including exotic species like spider monkeys, is governed by animal welfare laws and regulations. These laws might cover things like standards for housing, veterinary care, enrichment, and transportation. Laws pertaining to animal welfare must be followed by pet owners in order to protect their spider monkey companions.

Moral Aspects to Take into Account:

When owning spider monkeys as pets, pet owners have ethical duties to take into account in addition to legal ones. Concerns about these exotic animals' welfare, conservation, and moral treatment fall under the broad category of ethical considerations. Important moral considerations consist of:

Welfare Requirements: To maintain their wellbeing in captivity, spider monkeys have intricate physical, social, and psychological requirements that must be satisfied. Pet owners have a moral duty to meet the welfare needs of their monkey companions by giving them suitable housing, food, enrichment, and medical attention.

Conservation of Species: Due to habitat loss, poaching, and other threats, spider monkeys are considered vulnerable or endangered. The impact of captivity on wild populations and the state of spider monkey conservation should be taken into account by pet owners. Responsible ownership entails refraining from buying animals that have been captured in the wild, supporting conservation initiatives, and promoting the preservation of habitat.

Socialization and Enrichment: Spider monkeys are gregarious creatures that need chances for mental and physical stimulation, as well as social interaction. In order to support their monkey companions' natural behaviors and overall wellbeing, pet owners should place a high priority on socialization and enrichment activities.

Lifelong Commitment: Owning pet spider monkeys is an ongoing commitment that calls for time, money, and careful maintenance. Spider monkeys can live up to 20 years in captivity, so pet owners need to be ready to commit the necessary time, money, and emotional resources to provide for them.

Optimal Methods for Conscientious Ownership:

Respecting the law, maintaining moral principles, and putting the wellbeing of the creatures under your care first are all necessary components of responsible spider monkey ownership. Owners of pets can exhibit responsible pet ownership by:

- learning about the behavior, natural history, and maintenance needs of spider monkeys prior to obtaining a pet.

- supplying spider monkeys with large, well-furnished living quarters that satisfy their physical, social, and psychological needs.

- providing spider monkeys with a healthy, balanced diet that is catered to their individual dietary needs and preferences, all under the supervision of a licensed veterinarian or nutritionist.

- delivering routine veterinary care, which includes wellness examinations, immunizations, prevention of parasites, and fast handling of any health problems.

- utilizing positive reinforcement training methods with spider monkeys to encourage cooperative behavior, mental stimulation, and the development of trust.

- Supporting respectable conservation groups, taking part in advocacy campaigns, and spreading knowledge about the difficulties faced by wild populations are all ways to advocate for the welfare and conservation of spider monkeys.

- recognizing and honoring each spider monkey's unique requirements and preferences, as well as their social interactions, cues for communication, and behavioral patterns.

- avoiding the acquisition or ownership of spider monkeys that were captured in the wild and lending support to respectable breeders or rescue groups that place an emphasis on the well-being and moral treatment of animals.

- Making plans for the future and long-term care of the spider monkeys under your care, including measures to ensure their well-being in the event of illness, move, or other unanticipated events.

- acting as representatives for the welfare of exotic animals and spider monkeys by encouraging ethical ownership, informing people about their needs, and fighting for their preservation.

The keeping of spider monkeys as pets involves both ethical and legal obligations. Pet owners are required to respect ethical norms, negotiate a convoluted regulatory environment, and give the welfare and conservation of these remarkable animals top priority. Pet owners can guarantee a happy and responsible relationship with their monkey companions by following the law, encouraging moral ownership behaviors, and speaking up for the welfare of spider monkeys. Living with a spider monkey can be a fulfilling and enriching experience for both the animal and its human caregivers if done with thoughtful thought, devotion, and a commitment to compassionate stewardship.

Chapter 8

Common Obstacles to Overcoming When Keeping Spider Monkeys as Pets

Although owning a spider monkey as a pet can be rewarding, there are certain difficulties involved. Owning a spider monkey involves commitment, understanding, and tolerance for everything from tending to their intricate dietary and social requirements to dealing with behavioral problems and giving them the right medical attention. In order to maintain the wellbeing and happiness of spider monkeys kept in captivity, we will examine some of the typical problems encountered by pet owners in this thorough guide and offer workable solutions.

Nutritional Difficulties:

In order to preserve their health and vitality, spider monkeys have specific dietary needs that must be satisfied. It can be difficult for pet owners to provide their animals a healthy, well-balanced diet that corresponds with their innate food preferences. Typical dietary difficulties consist of:

Limited Food Availability: It can be difficult to find a wide range of fresh fruits, vegetables, nuts, and seeds all year round, particularly in areas where access to exotic produce is restricted.

Nutritional imbalance: Spider monkeys need a diet that is rich in vitamins and minerals, low in fat, and high in fiber. Without the right direction, it can be difficult to meet their nutritional needs and make sure they get all the nutrients they need.

Dietary Preferences: Pet owners must take into account the dietary preferences and aversions that each spider monkey may have. Dietary obstacles can be addressed by offering a wide variety of options and encouraging them to try new foods.

Techniques for Overcoming Nutritional Obstacles:

- To create a diet plan specifically designed for spider monkeys, speak with a trained veterinarian or nutritionist who specializes in primate care.

- To guarantee a varied and nutritionally balanced diet, find out where to buy fresh fruits, vegetables, and other staple foods in your area.

- To ensure that all necessary nutrients are received and to add variety to the diet, offer a range of fruits, vegetables, nuts, and seeds.

- To increase food appeal and promote consumption, try presenting food in different ways, such as chopping, slicing, or blending.

- Keep a close eye on the monkey's food intake and modify the diet as necessary to suit their preferences and nutritional needs.

Socialization Difficulties:

Being with their own kind, spider monkeys are gregarious creatures that enjoy each other's company. It can be difficult to give captive monkeys enough opportunities for socialization, particularly for those who only have one pet. Typical socialization difficulties consist of:

- Loneliness and Isolation: When left alone without the company of their conspecifics, spider monkeys may suffer from social isolation and loneliness. Depression, behavioral problems, and boredom can result from a lack of social interaction.

- Dominance and Aggression: It can be difficult to introduce new monkeys or integrate them into an established social group, which can result in dominance conflicts, aggression, and social tension.

- Inappropriate Social Behavior: When interacting with conspecifics or strangers, spider monkeys may display inappropriate social behaviors like fear, aggression, or territoriality.

Methods for Overcoming Socialization Difficulties:

Whenever possible, offer conspecifics the chance to socialize with one another through supervised play sessions, introductions to compatible individuals, or exposure to other monkeys' sounds and sights.

Use strategies for positive reinforcement and gradual introductions to help with socialization and lower the likelihood of aggression or conflicts over dominance.

Provide socially engaging enrichment activities, like grooming sessions, cooperative feeding, or shared playtime with interactive toys.

Keep a close eye on the monkey's social interactions and step in if aggression or inappropriate behavior arises. If necessary, seek advice from a certified primatologist or animal behaviorist.

To give your spider monkey company and social support, think about adopting or fostering a companion monkey from a respectable primate sanctuary or rescue group.

Conduct Issues:

Spider monkeys are perceptive, clever creatures with intricate behavioral requirements. Comprehending the innate behaviors of captive animals and facilitating their expression through suitable channels are essential for resolving behavioral issues. Typical behavioral issues consist of:

Stereotypic Behaviors: In reaction to stress, boredom, or a lack of environmental stimulation, spider monkeys may exhibit stereotypical behaviors such as pacing, self-harm, or excessive grooming.

Destructive Behaviors: When bored or irritated, spider monkeys may resort to destructive behaviors like biting, chewing on furniture, or throwing objects.

Fear and Anxiety: Spider monkeys may exhibit defensive, withdrawing, or aggressive behaviors in response to environmental, behavioral, or social changes.

Methods for Getting Past Behavioral Obstacles:

Create an environment that is rich and stimulating, allowing for natural behaviors, exploration, and mental stimulation. Foraging, puzzle feeders, climbing structures, and other sensory stimulation activities are examples of enrichment activities that can help reduce boredom and lower the likelihood of stereotypical behaviors.

To reduce stress and anxiety, create a routine and environment that are predictable. For spider monkeys, regularity in social interactions, feeding schedules, and enrichment activities fosters security and predictability.

Engage in enrichment activities, cooperate with others, and maintain composure by using positive reinforcement training techniques. Rewarding positive associations and encouraging learning can be achieved by providing treats, praise, or access to preferred activities in exchange for good behavior.

Keep a close eye on the monkey's behavior and act quickly to address any indications of stress, fear, or aggression. In order to help the monkey feel safe and secure in their surroundings, recognize and eliminate any anxiety or fear triggers and offer comfort and support.

If behavioral issues worsen or persist, consult a trained animal behaviorist or expert on primates. To address particular issues, a professional can carry out a behavior assessment, create a plan for behavior modification, and offer tailored recommendations.

Challenges in Veterinary Care:

Access to competent and experienced veterinarians specializing in exotic animals is necessary for providing spider monkeys with the necessary veterinary care. Concerns about medical care, emergency veterinary services, and preventive care may arise for pet owners. Typical difficulties in veterinary care include:

Restricted Access to Exotic Animal Veterinarians: It can be difficult to locate licensed veterinarians with expertise in exotic animal care and primate medicine, particularly in rural or isolated regions.

Needs for Preventive Care: In order to keep themselves healthy and happy, spider monkeys need to have regular veterinary exams, vaccinations, parasite control, and dental care. It can be difficult to find veterinarians who are interested in providing preventive care and who are knowledgeable about primate medicine.

Emergency Veterinary Services: It can be challenging to get timely, specialized veterinary care for spider monkeys in the event of a medical emergency. Timely treatment may be hampered by the scarcity of emergency veterinary clinics or specialists with training in primate medicine.

Methods for Overcoming Difficulties in Veterinary Care:

Before purchasing a spider monkey, do your homework and get in touch with a licensed exotic animal veterinarian or veterinary clinic that specializes in primate medicine. Check their qualifications, experience, and availability for both regular and urgent care.

Plan on having your spider monkey examined on a regular basis to keep an eye on their health, take care of any preventive care requirements, and build a rapport with the veterinarian. Talk about immunization schedules, dental care, preventing parasites, and any particular health issues or concerns for spider monkeys.

Based on your veterinarian's recommendations, create a veterinary care plan that includes regular checkups, vaccinations, prevention of parasites, and dental care. Maintain thorough records of your monkey's medical history, including shots, medications, and outcomes of diagnostic tests.

Create an emergency veterinary care plan that details how to get emergency services and provides contact details for wildlife rehabilitators, emergency veterinary clinics, and groups that rescue primates. In case of an emergency, be ready to take the monkey to the closest veterinary facility.

Learn about common health problems, preventative healthcare options, and how to treat spider monkeys in an emergency. Take part in educational seminars, workshops, or online forums to improve your understanding of veterinary management and primate care.

Although owning a spider monkey as a pet can be rewarding and enriching, there are certain difficulties that must be overcome in order to protect the happiness and well-being of these unusual creatures. Pet owners can give spider monkeys kept in captivity a loving and supportive environment by learning about their nutritional, social, behavioral, and veterinary care needs and putting into practice workable solutions for common problems. Pet owners can overcome obstacles and create a strong bond with their monkey companions by being patient, dedicated, and committed to responsible stewardship. This will foster a relationship based on mutual respect, trust, and understanding. Pet owners can create a positive and enriching experience for both the animals and their human caregivers by placing a high priority on the welfare and ethical treatment of spider monkeys.

Chapter 9

In conclusion, living with a spider monkey can be a rewarding experience.

Having a spider monkey as a pet is an amazing opportunity to create a special and meaningful relationship with one of nature's most fascinating animals, not just a responsibility. We have covered a wide range of topics in this guide, from understanding behavior and feeding requirements to handling socialization issues and giving appropriate veterinary care, all related to caring for spider monkeys. The experience of living with a spider monkey is incredibly fulfilling on many levels, even with the difficulties.

Establishing a Solid Bond:
Building a solid and meaningful relationship with your companion spider monkey is essential to the experience

of pet ownership. Pet owners can create a strong bond based on companionship, mutual trust, and understanding by placing a high value on positive interactions, exercises that build trust, and respect for one another. By engaging in common activities like playtime, grooming, and training sessions, pet owners and spider monkeys can create a bond that benefits both species and crosses species boundaries.

Promoting Well-Being and Enrichment:

A key component of ethical spider monkey care is enrichment, which offers chances for cognitive and motor development as well as for the expression of natural behavior. Pet owners can encourage well-being and prevent boredom, stress, and stereotypical behaviors by providing a stimulating environment that resembles the natural habitat of monkeys. Spider monkeys flourish when given a wide range of enrichment activities that are tailored to their specific needs and preferences, from socialization opportunities to foraging enrichment.

Fulfilling Particular Needs:

In order to maintain their health and well-being in captivity, spider monkeys have unique dietary, social, and behavioral requirements that must be satisfied. Pet owners can give their animals the proper care and accommodations that enhance their well-being by being aware of their natural history, behavior, and dietary needs. The special needs of spider monkeys in captivity are largely met by pet owners, whether it's by providing a balanced diet of fruits, vegetables, and nuts, facilitating social interactions with conspecifics, or using positive reinforcement training to address behavioral issues.

Encouragement of Advocacy and Conservation:

Advocates for the welfare and conservation of spider monkeys in the wild can benefit from the pet trade. Pet owners can help to preserve these endangered species and their natural habitats by educating the public about the difficulties faced by spider monkeys, supporting conservation efforts, and encouraging responsible ownership practices. Pet owners can encourage others to become stewards of wildlife and advocates for the protection of vulnerable species like spider monkeys through outreach, education, and advocacy programs.

Accepting the Trip:

Living with a spider monkey is an adventure full of happiness, difficulties, and memorable moments. As you work through the challenges of pet ownership and develop a relationship with your monkey partner, every day offers fresh chances for personal development, education, and understanding. The benefits of companionship, connection, and mutual affection far outweigh the inevitable obstacles and setbacks along the way, making pet ownership a profoundly fulfilling and life-changing experience.

Living with a spider monkey is a profound and fulfilling journey that benefits the animal as well as its human caregivers by bringing happiness, companionship, and enrichment. Pet owners can encourage the happiness and well-being of spider monkeys kept in captivity by providing a caring and supportive environment with dedication, compassion, and a commitment to responsible stewardship. Pet owners who embrace the opportunities and challenges of pet ownership can forge a lifelong bond with their monkey companions and set out on a journey of mutual love, growth, and discovery. The experience of taking care of a spider monkey can bring endless happiness and fulfillment, enhancing the lives of all those involved for years to come, provided they have the patience, understanding, and openness to learn.

Chapter 10

Common Questions (FAQs) Regarding Owning Spider Monkeys

- What is the legal standing for pet owners who own spider monkeys?

The legality of keeping a pet spider monkey differs depending on the jurisdiction. It may be necessary to obtain licenses or permits in many places in order to own exotic animals like spider monkeys. Before obtaining a spider monkey as a pet, it is imperative to learn about and comprehend the laws and regulations controlling the ownership of exotic animals in your community.

- For a spider monkey, what kind of enclosure is appropriate?

Spider monkeys need large, well-furnished enclosures that closely resemble their natural surroundings. To encourage natural behaviors and physical activity, the enclosure should have climbing frames, ropes, platforms, and hiding places. Additionally, it needs to be safe to keep the monkey from escaping and shield it from possible dangers.

- What foods do spider monkeys consume, and how can I feed them a healthy diet?

The main foods that spider monkeys eat are fruits, vegetables, nuts, seeds, and sometimes leaves and insects. A diverse and well-balanced diet that fulfills their dietary requirements for fiber, vitamins, minerals, and protein is imperative. Formulating an appropriate diet plan can be aided by speaking with a qualified nutritionist or veterinarian who specializes in primate care.

- Do spider monkeys require company and are they social animals?

Indeed, spider monkeys are gregarious creatures that prefer the company of other members of their own species. They can develop close relationships with human caregivers, but they also gain from interacting socially with other spider monkeys. If you are keeping a single monkey, it is advised to give them opportunities for socialization through supervised play sessions, introductions to matched people, or exposure to other monkeys both visually and auditorily.

- How can I help my spider monkey with behavioral issues?

In order to address behavioral issues with spider monkeys, one must comprehend their innate behaviors and provide them suitable channels for expression.

Unwanted behaviors can be reduced with the aid of enrichment activities, positive reinforcement training, and a stable schedule. To properly address particular behavioral issues, it might be necessary to consult with a qualified animal behaviorist or expert in primate behavior.

- What medical attention is required for a spider monkey?

For their health and wellbeing, spider monkeys need to have frequent veterinary examinations, vaccinations, parasite control, and dental care. To provide appropriate veterinary care, it is imperative to locate a licensed exotic animal veterinarian with experience in primate medicine. For spider monkeys to remain healthy over the long term, routine wellness examinations, diagnostic testing, and timely treatment of any health issues are essential.

- In captivity, how long do spider monkeys live?

In captivity, spider monkeys can survive for up to twenty-five to thirty years or longer with the right maintenance. Spider monkeys kept in captivity can live longer and be in better health if they are given access to veterinary care, social interaction, enrichment activities, and a healthy diet.

- If yes, how can I train my spider monkey?

It is possible to train spider monkeys to exhibit desired behaviors and promote cooperative interactions through the use of positive reinforcement techniques. Basic commands, enrichment activities, and husbandry tasks can all be covered in training sessions. Positive behaviors can be reinforced and the relationship between the monkey and its human caregivers strengthened by using rewards like praise, treats, or preferred activities.

- Which myths about owning a spider monkey are most prevalent?

Some common misconceptions about owning spider monkeys include thinking they are low-maintenance pets, thinking they can be kept alone, and underestimating their needs in terms of socialization, feeding, and behavior. Before obtaining a spider monkey as a pet, it is imperative to conduct extensive research and comprehend the duties and difficulties associated with ownership.

- What role can I play in the conservation of spider monkeys?

Contributing to conservation efforts requires funding credible conservation organizations, taking part in advocacy campaigns, and spreading knowledge about the state of spider monkey conservation and their natural habitats. Spider monkey conservation can also be supported by encouraging responsible ownership practices, opposing the purchase of animals taken from the wild, and supporting habitat protection programs.

Printed in Great Britain
by Amazon

55358433R00056